Ready...Set...
Tweet!

Ready...Set... Tweet!

A Speedy Guide to twitter

by Lou Belcher

Ready...Set...Tweet! A Speedy Guide to Twitter
by Lou Belcher

First Edition

Layout and design by
Suzanne Clements Graphic Design, LLC

Note: Technology for all of social media is rapidly changing. The author has made every effort to ensure that the instructions within this book are accurate and up to date as of the date of publication. There may be changes to Twitter by the time you read it. The author claims no responsibility for changes that have a bearing on this book after it is published. Subsequent editions will contain revisions to Twitter.

Dedicated to all who want to Tweet but don't know how.

Acknowledgements

Thanks to Jim Belcher, Hancel Deaton, and Kee Briggs for being my test audience. Special thanks to Suzanne Clements for the many ways her artistic and design talents touch my life.

Table of Contents

Chapter 12:

Resources:

Glossary:

Index:

Introduction

Why this book?

Just a little background

Technology today

Introduction:

Why this book?

For some strange reason, I took to Twitter like a cat to litter. You cat owners know what I mean. For the rest of you: you plop a kitten in litter once and it's good to go. That's the way it was for me and it surprised me. I know others haven't had that same experience.

So, I decided to share the mechanics of Twitter through this book. I'm going to keep it as short and sweet as I can. No need for long explanations, right? You just need to know what to do. And that's what I'm going to tell you. The rest you can learn with experience.

Just a little background

The emphasis on using Twitter to promote a website, product or service or to communicate with others on a formal or informal basis seems to be justified. People are gaining positive results from it. They are connecting with potential customers, clients or colleagues they would never encounter without Twitter.

Merely putting up a Twitter site and just leaving it there isn't enough. As with all good things, some work is involved. You can't put yourself on Twitter and hope people will come to you. They probably won't. You need to make yourself Twitter-worthy. It's not hard to do, but you need to commit yourself to it.

Twitter is a social media site. Marketing using social media is the hot topic of the moment and is liable to last a while. Without participating in it, you are missing out on one of the best, free-marketing tools around. However, it can be time consuming, so you must understand how to get the most out of it in the least amount of time. And, that's what I'm here to show you.

What's in *Ready...Set...Tweet!?*

Ready...Set...Tweet! is designed to help you get up and going on Twitter. To that end, it covers:

- how Twitter works
- how to set up and design your Twitter site
- page-by-page instructions on Twitter features
- how to Tweet
- followers and following
- putting it all together
- terminology

When following the instructions in this book to set up your Twitter site and to start Tweeting, don't be surprised if some of what you read is repetitious. There is some natural redundancy in *Ready...Set...Tweet!* In several instances the same information is needed in more than one section. To save you from having to flip back and forth while working on your Twitter site, key information is repeated where needed.

Technology today

There are a variety of web browsers available today. Do not be concerned if your web browser shows a Twitter page slightly different than shown in *Ready...Set... Tweet!* The major features will be the same and intuition will guide you.

Technology is changing quickly and with it Twitter will naturally make improvements and changes to its services. At the time of the publication of *Ready...Set... Tweet!* the contents of this book matched Twitter. Every effort will be made to revise *Ready...Set...Tweet!* when significant changes to Twitter occur.

Chapter 1:
What's All the Twitter About?

What is Twitter?

Twitter: The overall concept

**Purpose of Ready...Set...
Tweet!**

**Twitter is all about
communicating in a new way**

Along came Twitter...

Chapter 1: What's all the Twitter About?

I started hearing about Twitter in conjunction with the news. At the end of each segment, news anchors were urging me to join them on Twitter. I didn't really see much use for it until I was halfway through writing a book and wondered if Twitter could be helpful in marketing that book. Beyond that, I wondered if it could help me promote my blogs (I have four of them). So, I decided to sign on and see what Twitter was all about.

What is Twitter?

Technically, Twitter is classified as a micro-social media site on the Internet. It's a place where you can post messages to people who may be interested in your topic. What distinguishes it from other social media sites, such as *Facebook*, and why it is called a micro-social media site is that each message can be no more than 140 characters (including spaces).

I learned that overuse of Twitter is a possibility and under use of Twitter is a waste of time. Like Goldilocks, to make it worth your while, you need to get it just right. How do you go about doing that? By understanding what it can do for you and how—and by spending just enough time on it to get results without letting it consume your life.

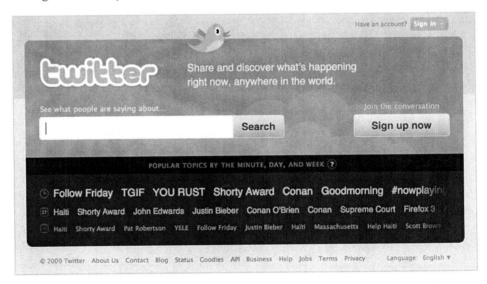

Twitter: The overall concept

Essentially, the concept of Twitter is strange if you think about it. You set up a page on this giant website and you start throwing 140-character messages out into cyberspace, hoping to attract followers. In the meantime, you visit other Twitter sites and click on a button to follow them in hopes that they will find you interesting enough to follow you back.

Confused? Yes, well, you won't be for long. After being on Twitter for a while now, I've pretty much figured out the basics of it, and I'm going to share my discoveries with you. Until we work our way through all the details, let me explain the basic concept. Twitter is a place to communicate, share, inform, and/or entertain like-minded people through 140-character messages. Beyond that, it becomes what you make of it.

Purpose of *Ready...Set...Tweet!*

Ready...Set...Tweet! is designed to give you the bare bones information about Twitter to help you get up and running quickly. There are lots of books that give in-depth explanation. This is not one of them. *Ready...Set...Tweet!* is intentionally short. It's the down-'n-dirty, get-to-the-point version. It is intended for those of you who just want to get going without all the hoop-la. I will not overload you with explanation in this book. You can get that elsewhere and later if you feel the need. Follow the steps in this book and get started on Twitter today.

Twitter is all about communicating in a new way

In the old days (about a year and a half ago, that is), when we wanted to get the word out about a product, service, event, or something that was happening in our lives, we would send email to a distribution list or we prepared costly paper items, such as brochures, booklets, posters, invitations, letters, newsletters, postcards, etc., and we would send them out to what we determined to be an interested audience. This often hit the spot, but it was costly and time consuming. If you didn't have the computer skills to put it all together, you had to hire someone to design and produce the poster, brochure, booklet, newsletter, etc. You had to pay the printer to print it and you had to pay postage to send your announcement.

Along came Twitter...

...and it's free. Except for accounting for the time you spend on it, you can get the word out without spending much money. Twitter can't fulfill all your marketing and communication needs, but it can spread the word fast and for many of us, that's all we need. The only folks you don't hit are those who aren't on Twitter. So that's a limitation, but even then, the advantage is that you have an infinite audience. You have access to people you may not have thought of as customers.

Chapter 2:
What Twitter Can Do for You

Common uses for Twitter

Chapter 2: What Twitter Can Do for You

Common uses for Twitter

Yesterday at lunch, a friend brought in a printed copy of a random page from Twitter because he wanted to show me something. Another fellow eating with us asked to see it. He had never been on Twitter and had determined from our talking about it that it was probably more intrusive than helpful. He likened it to being accosted by 25 or so co-workers in the hallway at work and not being able to hear any of them over the din of their collective voices.

I have four Twitter sites of my own and I manage a couple more for others. Two of my sites have over a thousand followers and are devoted to promoting writers and artists. The other two are for me. From the outside world, I have to admit that my friend might be right. Twitter might look like a bunch of folks throwing random thoughts to the wind. And to some, that perception remains because they don't delve into it far enough to see or reap the benefit of it. So, let's talk about the uses of Twitter and some of its benefits.

> A Tweet is the 140-character message you send out from your Twitter page. Tweet is also a verb that means the act of sending out the Tweet.

I, of course, can't go into all the specifics of uses people find for Twitter, but we'll hit the broad categories here. Within one or more of them you will, no doubt, see yourself.

Marketing

One of the most common uses of Twitter is to market a product or service. Businesses, large and small, use it to get the word out about what they do and to acquire customers or clients. Essentially, Twitter is a good place to put your name and the essence of your product or service before potential customers or clients. By Tweeting about what is happening with you and your product or service, you will keep potential customers up to date on what you are doing and about the possibilities of what you are presenting to the world. You may develop some sales just from these short messages you are sending into cyberspace.

Here is an example. If your company has a new product to present, write a blog post about it. Then go to Twitter and Tweet about your new post and your new product. Through your Tweets, you can also offer specials or discounts.

You would market a service through your Tweets in a similar manner. First, blog

about the new service, then Tweet about the blog. Or you could Tweet directly about the service. Both of these strategies raise awareness of what you have to offer. Remember to Tweet about other things most of the time to keep your followers interested.

Businesses use Twitter to get the word out about many different things. For example, they may use it to drive traffic to their websites or blogs in the manner we just discussed. However, this might not be for the sole purpose of selling something. Rather, business owners might just want to share some information with their customers.

Be careful with marketing Tweets. Intersperse other types of Tweets, so it doesn't look like you are only interested in selling.

Think through your strategy when using Twitter for marketing. I don't know about you, but the hard sell doesn't work on me. In fact, the harder you try to sell me something, the more determined I will become to not buy it. Many business owners have figured this out and have begun to give customers something for nothing. We all like that, don't we?

The "something" they are giving is information. They are packing their websites with useful information, tips, hints, (whatever you want to call it) to keep their customers engaged. And, to let their customers know when they've posted new information, they are Tweeting each time they put up a new post.

Mixed in with all those Tweets about the helpful information posted on the blog will be a Tweet about the actual product or service the person is selling. The followers of the blog and the Twitter site don't mind the occasional I've-got-to-sell-my- product Tweet as long as it occurs about 10% of the time.

Specific research
By reading the Tweets of others and by communicating with others on Twitter, you will be able to keep up to date on what is happening with your competitors. By following the Tweets of your competitors, you will learn what they are doing, the discounts and special deals they are offering, and their current approach. This should inform what you are doing as you will know what you are up against and can plan accordingly.

General research

By following those who are on the cutting edge in a field that interests you, you will keep up to date on what is going on in your field. Many Tweeters Tweet about new research they have found and will lead you to useful websites. Twitter is a great place for preliminary research on new topics. Through checking out who those you follow are following and who those who are the experts in the field are following, you will broaden your horizons. You naturally increase the possibility of remaining current in your field.

News organizations

Newspapers and television reporters use Twitter to gather the latest news faster than the speed of light. Some of the most recent top stories have been blown wide open because a pedestrian was in the right/wrong spot at the right time and Tweeted what happened. That Tweet was retweeted and the news agencies picked it up and the word spread.

Family, friends, and clubs

Many people use Twitter to keep in touch. Some of them have restricted accounts, so they can only talk to each other. Imagine receiving a Tweet that says, "It's a boy—8lbs, 10oz, healthy and Sarah is doing well..."

Twitter is also a good way for a club to make an announcement to members. You could, for example, set up a Twitter site for your garden club. You could use the Tweets to keep the others informed of upcoming meetings or events. You could do this on Twitter and allow anyone to follow the club and maybe find some new members amongst the people who follow you. Or, you could *Protect* your Tweets. This means that people have to request to follow you and only those who you grant access will see your Tweets. By using protected Tweets, you could give access to club members only and follow club members only. That way, you'll know when you go to Twitter that all the Tweets on your site will be about the garden club.

There are many psychological and emotional benefits that people derive from Twitter also. People form friendships on Twitter, share common interests, and find it comforting and fun to chat with others in this abbreviated and sometimes interrupted format.

Attention

Another psychological or emotional use for Twitter is that it's a way for people to gain attention from others without revealing all of themselves. Now, you might say this is cheating. There are, of course, those looking for attention at any cost. Most Twitter users chase them away by blocking them and Twitter itself is becoming more adept at throwing out people who are (spamming similar to those who send out spam by email) and those who send out risqué Tweets. Don't be shocked if you receive a random 140-character proposition. My advice is to block the person who sent it. If you're a guy, don't let your ego get all involved thinking it's real. It's probably just some guy trying to redirect you to a porn site or trying to sell you something. Don't give them the twisted attention they are seeking in such an inappropriate manner.

Announcements

Besides private announcements, there are plenty of public announcements going out over Twitter every day. As the editor of FloridaBookNews.com and BrevardArtNews.com, I Tweet daily about writers, artists and their events. If an artist has an opening reception for an exhibit, I Tweet about it. Or if an author gives a workshop or has a book signing, I Tweet about it. Hopefully the number of people who show up is larger due to the Tweets.

Collaboration

Many people work together through Twitter or find others to collaborate with through Twitter. And, you can't underestimate the power of Twitter to lend an ear. Many friendships form and many last because people find others of like interest with whom to communicate.

Other uses for Twitter

It's a place to post information that might be of help to others. There are people on Twitter who never actually Tweet to anyone in particular. They Tweet daily. They seem to not be selling or promoting anything. They just have a whole lot of information to share and want to tell it to somebody and it seems anybody will do.

As a writer, my favorites of these folks are the ones who put out a quotation a day. I love quotations by famous people. Isn't it perfect to make the quotations that are under 140 characters into Tweets?

Periodically, click on your followers. If you see any new ones who are obviously spammers or Tweeting about suggestive material, block them.

There are many more uses for Twitter. These few will give you some ideas. Before you set up your Twitter account, do some thinking about what you want to gain from it. Having a good idea of why you are going on Twitter will help you form a focused site to meet your needs.

page 22

Ready...Set...Tweet! A Speedy Guide to Twitter

Chapter 3:
How Twitter Works

How it works

How Twitter fits into this communication chain

Chapter 3: How Twitter Works

Twitter is a web-based phenomenon. It's important to understand how you can get the most out of it. So, let's go through what you'll need to make the most of Twitter.

If your reason for being on Twitter is just to chat with others, to keep up to date on what others are doing or to learn about a specific topic, you are probably good to go. Just follow the instructions to sign up for a Twitter page and begin following Tweeters of interest to you.

If you want to use Twitter for recreation or for gathering information, you don't need your own website or blog. You can exist on Twitter and get out of it what you want just by reading Tweets by others, going to the websites they recommend and Tweeting back to your followers.

However, if you want to draw attention to yourself, an organization, or a business; you'll probably want to set up a website or blog to interface with Twitter.

How it Works

Twitter, when used alone, is quite effective in communicating short bits of information and getting conversations started. It becomes even more powerful when combined with a website, a blog, a photo gallery or one of the many applications designed to enhance the scope and value of your message.

Website
It's good to have a website if what you are doing would benefit from a place on the Internet where you want to put information for others to reference and the information doesn't change very often.

Websites used to be the be all and end all. Today, most websites are a bit static. It's good to have a website to send people to as a destination for

- the deeper explanation of your product, service or topic
- your contact information
- the content that convinces the customer that their consideration

and pursuit of your product or service are worthwhile

- persuading your customers to return to see more and possibly buy on a subsequent visit.

If you're in business, your website is where you put information that won't change too often. Unless you are a computer whiz, you will probably need a graphic designer or computer geek to take care of your website. In that case, you will write something to put on your website, give it to your website designer, and you'd see it up in a few days.

Blog

Due to the labor needed to make changes to websites, people have turned to using blogs to put up daily or weekly information. This could include information to

- keep in touch with friends or family

- post information vital to a club or organization

- keep customers informed of changes in your business

- tell customers about new products or services you have to offer

- keep others informed on happenings in your industry

- inform customers of events that may be of interest, such as specials and discounts

- inform or entertain others about a favorite topic

Because websites were more time-consuming to update on a daily or weekly basis, the blog was invented and blogger services were set up. The blog essentially is a place where you can go to post daily, weekly, or minute-by-minute messages using words, pictures, videos or a combination of all three. In some cases, people use blogs as their total web presence. If they are in the business of selling a product or service, they connect the blog to a shop or just install buy buttons and they're in business.

There are many ways (through RSS feeds, through Search Engine Optimization, etc.) to entice visitors to your blog, but these pale in comparison to the effect

Twitter can have on traffic to your site. Ergo.., we enter the world of Twitter.

How Twitter fits into this communication chain

What a revelation when I discovered Twitter. I had heard of it for a while on TV. It was mostly mentioned on news programs. Eventually, I decided to go visit it myself. At the time, I had the art blog and the book blog that were gaining some popularity, but I wondered what Twitter could do for them.

So, one day I took the plunge. I decided to go to *http://Twitter.com* and see what all the chatter was about. To experiment, I set up a site for myself (called *@LouWrites*) and I sat there. I wasn't sure how to go about finding followers or how I could go about following others. But with some nosing around and putting key words (writing, writers, fabric art, quilting, etc.) in the search engine, I soon started finding some folks with like interests. I followed a few that first day and went back the next to see what they were saying about themselves and about the world. In the meantime, I was reading *Twitter Power* by Joel Comm. It was a good overall book that explained the origins and uses of Twitter.

Once I was on Twitter, it was easier to see from the inside how it all worked. So, I would recommend to you to start with your own Twitter site. Through it, you will get a feel for Twitter before setting up Twitter sites for your business ventures where you want it all to run smoothly from day one.

Just use a book such as *Ready... Set...Tweet!* and go through the steps of setting up your page. Don't use the prize name you've been saving for your important Twitter site. Rather, start one as a practice site. That way, you'll know what you're doing and won't look like a novice before potential customers and clients. And, you can always delete the practice site later if you want.

Anyway, Twitter is a way to encourage/nudge people to become interested in you and in your product or service without having to resort to the hard sell. You may need to do a bit of research to write your daily Tweets, but it will be worth it. You may want to Tweet a picture now and then, Tweet the link to someone else's website that contains some valuable or entertaining information about a common topic, write a Tweet that is a question to pull others into the conversation, etc.

After you Tweet about all these related things that are meant to be of value to

your followers, then you will post something to your blog and Tweet about it to send your Twitter followers to it….. Get it? You want your Tweets to be valuable and entertaining to your followers.

The chain of events works something like this:

- you post something to your blog or website
- you Tweet about your post with a link to your post in the Tweet
- followers of your Twitter site read your Tweet
- those who read your Tweet click on the link to your blog post or website
- your followers read your blog post or website and comment on what you've said.

The preparation of the website or blog post and the Tweet may take some time, but it'll be worth it. Allow yourself whatever time you have each day and put that into creating a list of interesting Tweets for the day.

Chapter 4:
Ready?

Determining the topic for your Twitter site

Getting your ducks in a row before signing on to Twitter

Chapter 4: Ready?

Determining the topic for your Twitter site

It's important to determine the right topic for your Twitter sight. You don't want it to be so broad that potential followers can't pin it down to know whether to follow you. For example, you don't want your Twitter site to be about wild animals if you will be Tweeting only about polar bears. People who are interested in tigers or elephants will lose interest.

Conversely, you don't want to make your topic so specific that you have difficulty finding followers. Here are some things to consider when deciding on a topic for your Twitter site:

1. Why do you want a Twitter site?
2. If you have a blog and are hoping to send people to your blog, make the topic of your Twitter site match your blog. That's an easy answer.
3. If you want a broader Twitter site than your blog, so you'll be able to reach more people, define your Twitter site accordingly.

Once you've determined a topic, carefully choose a name for your Twitter site. Be concrete with the name rather than cute. Cute might grab the attention and tickle some readers, but concrete will attract those followers really interested in your topic.

Getting your ducks in a row before signing on to Twitter

Before signing on to Twitter for your business or avocation, be sure you have your ducks in a row. They are:

1. Determine why you want a Twitter account.
   What are you intending to do with it?
2. If you are intending to use Twitter to drive traffic to your website or blog, be sure to set up your website or blog first. If you already have a website or blog, be sure to check it over to make sure it looks the way you want it to look and communicates what you want it to communicate before you sign on to Twitter.
3. Determine the topic of your Twitter site.

4. Determine a good name for your Twitter site.

Once you've accomplished this list, you are ready for Twitter.

Ready...Set...Tweet! A Speedy Guide to Twitter

Chapter 5:
Signing Up for Twitter

Sign-up page

Almost finished

Finished

Chapter 5: Signing Up for Twitter

It's easy to sign up for Twitter. Here are the steps:

1. Open a web browser.

2. Go to http://Twitter.com

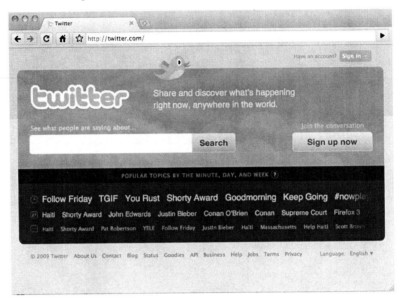

3. Click on *Sign up now*.

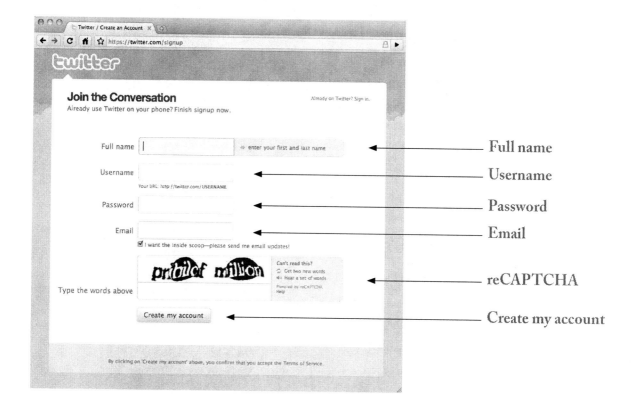

Sign-up page

- **Full name:**

  Enter your real name (or the name of your company or group) in the top box. As you enter your real name (or the name of your company or group), Twitter will check for availability. You will see the result of this check to the right of the space. Revise your choice for *Full name* as necessary.

- **Username:**

  In the second box, enter the *Username* you have chosen for your Twitter site. If you are going to use your real name as your username, enter that. This will become the address for your website. If you are going to be tweeting for your business, you will probably want to enter the name of your business as your username. Do not put spaces between words and do not choose a username that is over 15 characters. As you enter your chosen username, Twitter will check for availability and you will see the result of this check to the right of the space where you entered your choice. Revise your choice as necessary.

- **Password:**

  Choose any *password*. The Twitter sign-up sheet tells you in the right-hand column if you have chosen a good password or not. Choose a *very strong password*. Write it down in a secure location, so you'll be able to get back into your Twitter site when you go to sign in.

- **Email:**

  Fill in your *email address*. If you have more than one email address, choose the one you want to use for your Twitter correspondence and fill it in here. There is a check mark under this area. If you leave the check mark, you will receive email updates about Twitter. If you click on the check mark, it will disappear and you will not receive the updates. It's your choice.

- **reCAPTCHA:**

  Type in what you see. This is a test to make sure you are a human and not some computer program trying to sign up.

- **Create My Account:**

  You're almost done. Click on *Create My Account*.

Almost finished

After you click *Create My Account*, you will land on *Find sources that interest you.*

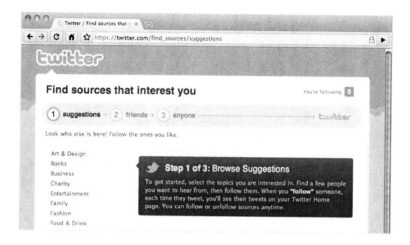

1. Find sources that interest you.

This is a page that lists topics. Click on a topic of interest and you will see a list of Twitter sites that might be of interest to you. Click on the icon to the right of the site of interest to follow that site. I recommend that you hold off on this. I have found that it's much better to set up your Twitter page before your start following others. When you are finished on this page or if you want to skip this page, click on *Next step: friends* at the bottom of the page.

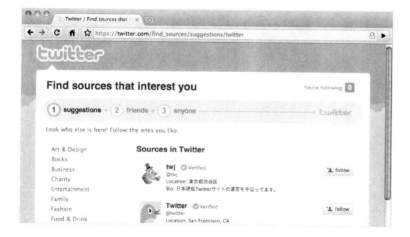

2. Friends.

After you click on *Next step: friends*, you will land on a page where Twitter will offer to search your email address books for people for you to follow on Twitter. It's up to you whether you want to do this or not. Personally, I like to pick and choose who I will follow, and I'll show you how to do this later in the book. If you don't want Twitter to search your address books for people to follow or if you have completed having Twitter search your email, go to the bottom of the page and click on the words, *Next step: others.*

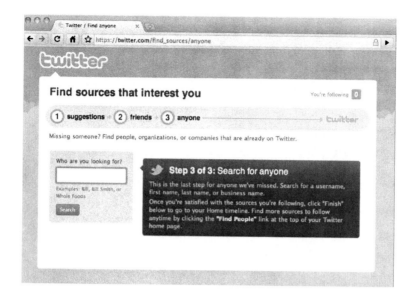

3. Next step: anyone.

After you click on *Next step: others*, you will land on a page where you can search by first name, last name, username, or business name for people to follow. Again, I would hold off on this until you have your Twitter site set up. When you are finished with this page, click on, *Nest step: You're done!*

Finished

When you click on *Next step: You're done!* you will land on your Twitter page. The first order of business is to *Confirm Your Account*. Across the top of your page, you will see a banner that will direct you to go to your email account. Do so and click on the link in the email you just received from Twitter. This will confirm your account.

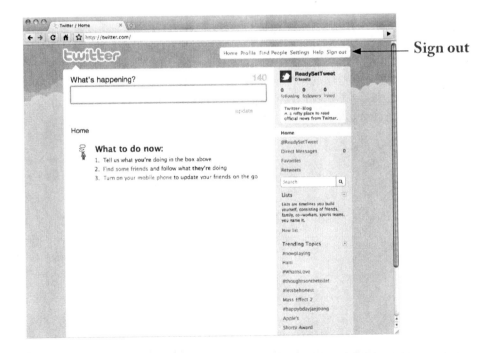

Twitter account confirmation Inbox | X

Twitter to me · · · · · · · · · · · · show details 10:25 AM (19 minutes ago) · Reply ▾

Images are not displayed.
Display images below -
Always display images from twitter-confirmation-readysettweet=gmail.com@postmaster.twitter.com

Hi, ReadySetTweet

To confirm your Twitter account, please verify that this email address
(readysettweet@gmail.com) belongs to you by clicking this link:
http://twitter.com/account/confirm_email/ReadySetTweet/GDBDC-B3H38

Thanks! The Twitter Team

We ask you to confirm your account for security reasons. Learn more

↰ Reply → Forward

Congratulations, you are now signed up for Twitter. If you have had enough for one day, you can quit by going to the upper right-hand corner of the page and clicking on *Sign out*. If not, you can get started in Chapter 6.

Sign out

Chapter 6:
The Features of Your Twitter Page

Signing in

Learning your Twitter pages

Chapter 6: The Features of Your Twitter Page

You get up in the morning, do your exercises, run around the block, make a cup of coffee and sit down at your computer. Yesterday, you followed the directions in Chapter 5 and you successfully signed up for a Twitter account. That was enough for one day, but today you are ready to finish getting set up on Twitter.

Signing in

Sign in to Twitter

If you've been using Twitter from your phone, click here and we'll get you signed up on the web.

Username or email

Password   Forgot?

☐ Remember me

Sign In

There are two ways to sign in.

1. One is to open a web browser and type in *http://Twitter. com*. Click on the *Sign in* button. A form will come up and will ask for your *Uusername or email* and your *Password*. You wrote this information down yesterday when you signed up. Where did you put that piece of paper? Once you find it, type in the information and click on the *Sign in* button below it.

2. The second way to sign in is to open a web browser and type in your Twitter URL. For me that would be *http://Twitter.com/ LouWrites*. For you, that would be *http://Twitter.com/yourusername*. You will land on your Twitter page. Click on *Sign in* and type in your *Username or email* and *Password*, then click on *Sign in*.

Using either method, you will see *Remember me* above the *Sign in* button. Click on the box if you want the computer to remember your *Sign in* information. When you click on *Sign in*, you will land on your *Home* page on Twitter.

Learning your Twitter pages

To familiarize you with items of the menu bar at the top of the page, we'll go on a quick tour of each of them, so you will know the purpose of each.

Twitter menu bar

To start, look at the top of the page on the right side. There you will find the words *Home, Profile, Find People, Settings, Help* and *Sign out*. Below is a short description of each of these. Later, we will go into a longer description including all the details about each of the pages these words represent.

Home

The *Home* page is an active page of your Twitter site. By this I mean that it is a page where you Tweet and where you see all the Tweets (in real time) of those you are following or of people who are specifically Tweeting to you. Every time one of the people you are following Tweets, the Tweet appears at the top of the list of Tweets on this page. Your Tweets will be posted chronologically to this list as well.

If you are following only one or two people, the Tweets will not move down the page very fast. Slowly, they will progress down the page whenever someone (you or one of those you are following) posts a Tweet.

Conversely, the Tweets will move faster down this page if you are following lots of people. For example, if you are following 1,000 people, the Tweets will move quite quickly because more people are Tweeting.

When you are following lots of people, you will probably find that any one Tweet will stay visible on the page for maybe a minute or two, depending on how active those people are. I'm telling you this so you won't be frustrated if no one responds to you each and every time you Tweet. It just might be that no one was paying close attention during that brief period of time. So, I guess what I'm advising is to avoid the drama and don't take anything too seriously. Later, we'll go into ways to gain the attention of those who are following you.

Home **Profile** Find People Settings Help Sign out

Profile

The *Profile* page is the page that shows only your Tweets. They are listed on this page in chronological order from the most recent to the earliest. This is the page visitors to your Twitter page will see (they don't see your *Home* page). It is also the page where the active link to your website or blog will be listed. You won't see the link on the *Home* page. It occurs here in the sidebar so that your visitors will be able to go to your website or blog to check you out when they are making a decision whether they want to follow you or not or if they want to gain information about what you are up to.

Your visitors can go to your *Profile* page and scroll through your Tweets from most recent backward if they want. Most visitors will only look at your last Tweet or two and then go to your website or blog to determine if they want to follow you.

Home Profile **Find People** Settings Help Sign out

Find People

The *Find People* button will take you to a search page. The search page gives you four different ways to find people on Twitter. We'll go into each of these later. For now, they are (from right to left):

1. Find on Twitter

2. Invite by email

Before you sign off Twitter, take a look at your Profile page to see if your most recent Tweets are ones you want visitors to notice first.

3. Find Friends

4. Browse Suggestions

Home Profile Find People <u>Settings</u> Help Sign out

Settings

Click on the *Settings* button when you want to go to the page to set up how your page will look, to enter your website or blog information, to upload a picture for your avatar (that's the little picture that represents you and goes out with every Tweet you send) and to upload a background and work on the design of your Twitter page. There are several pages related to *Settings*. We'll discuss those in detail later, too.

Home Profile Find People Settings <u>Help</u> Sign out

Help

The *Help* button will take you to a help area where you can type in a term or question. A search engine will pull up answers to that question.

Home Profile Find People Settings Help <u>Sign out</u>

Sign Out

Click on the *Sign out* button when you are finished using Twitter for the session or for the day.

Ready...Set...Tweet! A Speedy Guide to Twitter

Chapter 7:
Setting Up Your Twitter Page

Account

Password

Mobile

Notices

Picture

Design

Chapter 7: Setting Up Your Twitter Page

On your *Home* page, click on *Settings* to go to the area where you can set up and change the look of your Twitter site in order to make it your own.

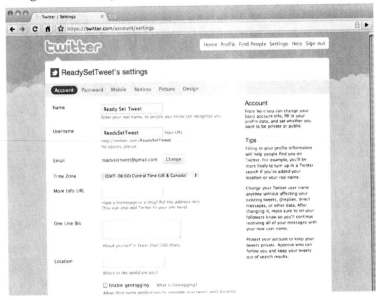

> If you are going to want to send people to your blog, be sure to set that up before you start Tweeting.

You'll want to do at least some of this before you start following people. When you start following people, they will naturally go to your Twitter page to see if they want to follow you as well. So, it's important to make your Twitter page look as complete and professional as possible.

It's not necessary to have a blog or website to correspond to your Twitter site. It's up to you. However, if you are setting up a blog or a website at the same time that you are setting up a Twitter site, it's best to set up the blog/website first.

Don't rush the process. You don't want people going to your blog/website before it's ready, so plan to set up your Twitter site after your blog/website looks the way you want it to. And put up a couple of good blog posts before you start Tweeting and sending people to your blog site. When they reach it, you want them to find something interesting to read.

So, when you are ready to set up your Twitter page, click on *Settings*. Many people design their Twitter page to look similar to their website so that the branding is in sync. This is not a bad idea. People will remember that the two are tied together and may remember you for presenting a harmonious front.

Take your time in setting up your Twitter page so that it's just the way you want it when people stop by to see you. When setting up your Twitter page, don't be afraid of the *Settings* functions.

For those of you who are a bit intimidated by the computer: Be brave! You can do one thing on the *Settings* page and stop there if it makes you nervous. No need to set it up all at once if you get the feeling it'll explode with each push of the *Save* button. Do a little, then come back later to do a little more. You'll become bolder with each session. You can click on the *Save* button at the bottom of the page at any time. That will save your changes, and you can continue the next time you sign in.

The final word on intimidation... There is probably nothing you can do when setting up your page that you can't undo later. Therefore, have at it, relax and follow the steps below. I'll explain each in some detail. If you don't need that much explanation, it won't hurt my feelings if you skip some of the text. So, here we go.

Account

Home Profile Find People Settings Help Sign out

Click on the word *Settings* at the top of the *Home* page or *Profile* page on your Twitter site. This will take you to the page under *Settings* called *Account* where you will set up the information that will appear on your *Profile* page. Fill in the following information:

> Name
>
> Ready Set Tweet
>
> Enter your real name, so people you know can recognize you.

- **Name:**
  Enter you real name or if you don't want your real name on it, enter the name of your Twitter site.

Explanation:

The instructions say to enter your real name so people can find you. This is okay if it's a personal account, but I have blog accounts that aren't about me. Therefore, a couple of my Twitter accounts don't need my name on the Twitter page. I put the name of the blog in the *Name* space to ensure I'm not the topic of the Twitter page. For example, one of my blogs is *BrevardArtNews. com*. It's not important for people to know my name, so I put *Brevard Art News* in for the Twitter *Name* for that account. On my personal account, however, I put in *Lou Belcher* as my *Name*.

● **Username:**
You signed up with a *Username* and will probably use that here.

Explanation:

If this is a personal account, you may want to use your name as the *Username*; but it will be the URL for Twitter, so don't use spaces. For the arts Twitter account, I have *BrevardArtNews* as the *Username*. That makes my Twitter URL *http://Twitter.com/brevardartnews*. If I chose to use my name, the URL would be *http://Twitter.com/loubelcher*. If you are using this Twitter account to promote your business, it's probably best to use some form of the name of the business to make it easy for people to search for you on Twitter. Remember, you can only use 15 characters for the *Username* and no spaces.

● **Email:**
Enter the *Email* address where you want to receive email from Twitter. You have three choices:

1. Have the email from Twitter sent to your email account.
2. Open a free email account with one of the service providers, such as yahoo or gmail, and use it just for Twitter.
3. Choose not to receive email from Twitter.

Explanation:

Choose wisely on this. All the email for your Twitter account will be sent to whatever email address you insert here. You may want to set up a separate email account just for Twitter because you will receive all direct messages and you'll receive an email each time someone signs on to follow you. This is a lot of email when you are initially gathering followers. If you think that you won't want to attend to the mail each day, set up a separate email account for your Twitter site so your important emails don't get lost in the Twitter notices.

There is a *Change* button next to the space where you entered your email address. Click on this to change your email address if needed.

Time Zone | (GMT−05:00) Eastern Time (US & Canada)

• Time Zone:

Click on this and choose the right time zone for where you live.

More Info URL | www.readysettweet.com
Have a homepage or a blog? Put the address here.
(You can also add Twitter to your site here)

• More Info URL:

Type in the URL of your blog or website here to send people there to read more about you or your topic.

Explanation:

If you have a blog or a website, you'll probably want to connect it to your Twitter page. Put the URL of your blog or website here. This web address will appear on your profile page and it will be active for your visitors to click through to your blog or website. At the beginning of the address, be sure to type *http://*. Twitter addresses don't appear active unless you use the full address, such as *http://brevardartnews.com*.

If you don't have a website or blog but do have an on-line shop or a photo account on one of the gallery sites, such as Flickr, you could use the URL for that site in the *More Info URL* space.

If you aren't interested in sending followers to any sites, leave this space blank.

- **One Line Bio:**

Type a one-line bio (160 characters) here. It will appear on your Profile page to tell readers about you or the topic of your Twitter page.

Explanation:

Before you fill out this section, think carefully what you want to tell people about yourself. You have 160 characters to tell visitors why you are on Twitter and what you'll include in your Tweets. You don't want to merely say, "I love to Tweet" or something like that. You want, in those few words, to convey what it is about you, your Tweets and your website that should interest people and what you might have in common with those who visit you.

So, be sure to get to the point with your *One Line Bio* and tell people what you are all about. Here are a couple of examples. For http://Twitter.com/LouWrites, I say, *"Writer, editor, photographer. I write, edit and consult on book-length fiction, nonfiction and blogging."* The *One Line Bio* for Brevard Art News says, *"Brevard Art News is a blog dedicated to keeping people in Florida and beyond informed about the artists of this area and what they are doing."*

Remember, you only have 160 characters, so make each word count. If necessary, it's okay to make it a list of key words for your topic rather than complete sentences. Write so people will get the point.

Location	Florida

Where in the world are you?

☐ Enable geotagging   What is Geotagging?

Allow third party applications to annotate your tweets with location information.

Delete all location data

Delete all historical location data from your tweets. The process can take up to 30 minutes.

- **Location:**

List where you live, if you want to.

You can be as specific or as general as you want to be with this. I live in Florida and that is what I put in for my *Location* on my personal account. Some tweeters include the city, too. Some say *The World*. It just depends on how comfortable you are about having those folks who follow you know your location.

Under this item there is also a box (to check or not check) called *Enable geotagging*. If you click this box, it will reveal more specific information about your location. There are words to the side of this that say *What is Geotagging?* Click on these words to learn more in order to make your own decision. In this same area is a button called: *Delete all location data.* This button allows Twitter to delete all historical location data from your Tweets.

Language	English ⇕
	What language would you like to Twitter in?

• Language:

I chose English. You can choose whatever language you are most comfortable with.

☐ Protect my tweets
Only let people whom I approve follow my tweets. If this is checked, you WILL NOT be on the public timeline. Tweets posted previously may still be publicly visible in some places.

• Protect my tweets:

I suggest that you leave this blank unless you don't want anyone to see your tweets without applying to you for permission.

Explanation:

In my view, the point of being on Twitter is to gain attention. In order to do that, your Tweets need to be visible to those who come to your Twitter site. Otherwise, how will they determine if they want to follow you? If you protect your Tweets, people will have to apply to you to be invited in.

Frankly, when I see one of the signs on someone's site that their Tweets are protected, I move on. I figure if they want me to see their tweets, they would leave them open to be seen.

Now, there is a legitimate use for checking the *Protect my tweets* button. If you go onto Twitter as part of a club or with several pals and you only want to Tweet to each other and to those you invite into your select group, then yes, click on *Protect my tweets* to ensure privacy of your group.

• Save:

Click *Save* to save your responses to the items on this page.

Explanation:

Once you have filled out the page the way you want it, click *Save*. All the additions and changes you have made will be saved. You can also save any time in the process of filling it out. It will save what you have done so far, and you can come back and do more later.

After saving, it is wise to return to the *Profile* page and check your work. Look in the upper right-hand sidebar. You'll see your name or the name of your Twitter page, your location, the web address that your page will click to (click on the address to ensure that it goes to that address. If it doesn't, go back to the *Account* page and correct the address), and your bio (read through it to ensure there are no errors). Go back to the *Account* page and make corrections as needed and click on *Save* to save them.

• Delete my account

If you decide to delete your account, click on the words *Delete my account* in the bottom left corner of the Account page.

Password

The next tab on the Settings page is *Password*. This is where you can change your password if desired. It's self-explanatory. Just fill in the spaces and click on *Change*.

Mobile

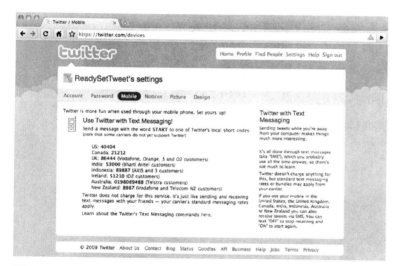

The next tab on the *Settings* page is *Mobile*. This tells you how to Tweet from your mobile phone through texting. Full instructions on this are provided under this tab, so I won't spend time here explaining it again.

Notices

The next tab on the *Settings* page is *Notices*. On this page you can choose what notices you want to receive from Twitter by email. You have three choices. They are:

- *New Follower Email*. Receive an email each time someone starts following you.

- *Direct Text Email*. Receive an email each time someone you follow sends you a direct message.

- *Email Newsletter*. Receive emails from Twitter to keep you up to date.

After you make your choices, click *Save*.

Picture

The next item on the *Settings* page is *Picture*. This is where you upload a picture to use as your avatar on Twitter. It's good to prepare the picture before you upload it. Or, you can upload different pictures until you find a look you want.

Many people use actual pictures of themselves. Others use pictures or icons to represent themselves. As you may have noticed, I have this flower theme going on. (@LouWrites has my signature sunflower as the avatar, @BrevrdArtNews has a macro photo of a sunflower center, and @FloridaBookNews has a field of black-eyed Susans). If your emphasis on Twitter is a business, you may want to have a picture of you or use a picture of your logo.

When you prepare the picture, make sure it is a jpg, gif, or png file no larger than 700k. Prepare the picture as a square if you can as that's the shape of the picture space.

Here are the steps to putting your picture on Twitter as your avatar:

- Save a picture to your hard drive so it will be easy for you to find.

Browse... No file chosen
Maximum size of 700k. JPG, GIF, PNG.

- To upload the picture, click on the *Browse* button on the *Picture* page and find the picture file on your hard drive.

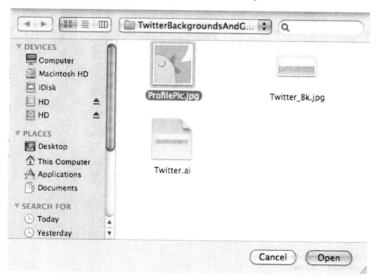

- When you find the picture, click on it and click on *Open*. The name of the route to that file will appear in the *Browse* window.

Choose File ProfilePic.jpg
Maximum size of 700k. JPG, GIF, PNG.

Save

- Once it appears, click on the *Save* button and wait. This usually doesn't take long, but be patient. You can click on your *Profile* page once the picture appears to check to see how you like it.

- If you don't like it, click on the *Delete current* button and start the process again.

Design

Chapter 8 deals with the design of the background and design colors for your Twitter page, so we will skip that here.

Chapter 8:
Changing Your Background

Twitter background themes

Design your own background

Change design colors

Chapter 8: Changing Your Background

The next item on the *Settings* page is *Design*. This is where you can change the background of your Twitter page to one of the designs offered by Twitter or you can change it to a background you make or have had made for you to match your website or blog.

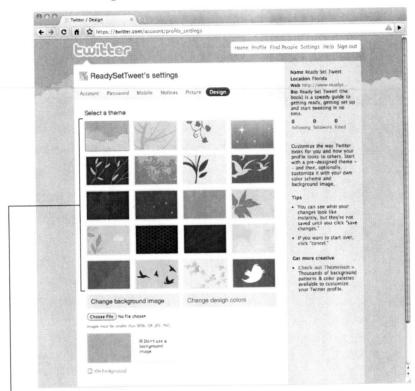

Twitter background themes

To try on different background themes provided by Twitter, follow these steps:

- When you are on your Twitter *Home* page, click on *Settings*.

- On the *Settings* page, click on *Design*.

- The squares on this page are samples of Twitter background themes.

- Click on a *theme* that you want to try and scroll to the

bottom of the page and click on *save changes*.

- Wait and you will see the new background.

- If you like it, click on *Home* to return to your Home page.

- If you don't like it, continue trying out different *themes* until you find one that you like. Remember to click on the *theme* and then click on *save changes* each time.

Design your own background

If you don't want to use any of the *themes* offered, you can use an image you design (or some talented friend designs) for your Twitter page. On *@LouWrites*, my Twitter background goes with my website: *http://www.LouBelcher.com.*

Here are the steps for making and uploading your own background:

- In Photoshop or some similar program, make the background image to measure approximately 1944 pixels wide by 1116 pixels high. The image must be jpg, gif or png format. Be careful with the overall size of this image. You must save it so it is under 800K in total size.

- Once you have designed a background that you like, save it on your hard drive so you will be able to find it easily.

Computer monitors are different sizes and shapes. When designing a background, keep the text close to the left edge to be sure all will see it.

Account   Password   Mobile   Notices   Picture   **Design**

- To try out your new background, go to the *Design* page in *Settings*.

Change background image

- Click on *Change background image*.

Browse... No file chosen
Images must be smaller than 800k. GIF, JPG, PNG.

- Click on the *Browse* button.

If you have a picture that will work well as a Twitter background when repeated, click on *tile background* when uploading the photo.

- Find the image of the custom background on your hard drive, click on it and click *Open*.

- The file route will appear in the window next to the *Browse* button.

save changes

- Click on *save changes* and wait for your background to appear.

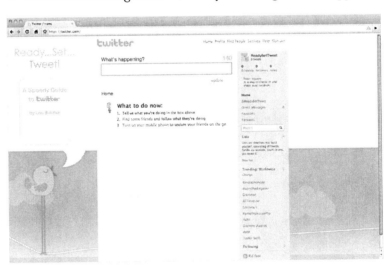

- Click on *Home* and see how you like it. It may take some tweaking until you get it the way you want.

Here are some tips on designing a good background:

- If you decide to put information about your website or your Twitter topic on your background, don't put anything of importance in the center of the background. It will not show, because the stream of tweets appears in the middle.

- Put any written information at the far left edge of the background and don't make the written information any wider than a business card because on smaller screens and laptops the words will go under the tweet stream.

- If you put your web address on the background, don't frustrate yourself by trying to make it active. Take a look at http://twitter.com/LouWrites (you can go there without having your page up). See how I have my web address (LouBelcher.com) on the left side of the background. It is not possible to make it so the reader can click to the website. However, it's not a bad idea to put it there for people to copy.

Change design colors

If you don't like the colors of other components of your page (such as the text, links, sidebar or sidebar border) with your new background, you may want to change those colors. To do so:

Change design colors

- Go back into *Design* and click on *Change design colors*. It will show you the colors you have for: *background, text, links, sidebar,* and *sidebar border*.

background	text	links	sidebar	sidebar border

- Choose the item you want to change by clicking on the box of its current color.

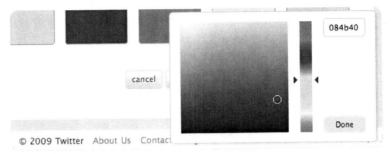

If you know hexadecimals, type the color code in the space to the right of the color selector to use a specific color.

- You'll see a box with gradations of colors and a strip with gradations of colors. Move the color selector around until you find the color value you want for the item.

save changes

- Once you find the color, click on *done* and then click *save changes* and the color of the item will change.

- Return to *Home* to see how the new color works.

Repeat the process as many times as necessary with each of the features until your page looks the way you want it to.

Then click *save changes*. Go to your *Profile* page or *Home* page and check to see that you are pleased with everything.

Chapter 9:
Functions on Each Part of Each Page

Home page

Profile page

Find people

Settings

Help

Sign out

Chapter 9: Functions on Each Part of Each Page

Until you sign on and begin using your Twitter site, this information may seem confusing. Read through it now just to become familiar with what is offered. After you have started to work on your Twitter site, read through it again carefully while looking at your computer screen. It'll make more sense then, and knowing what is offered on each page will help you get going faster.

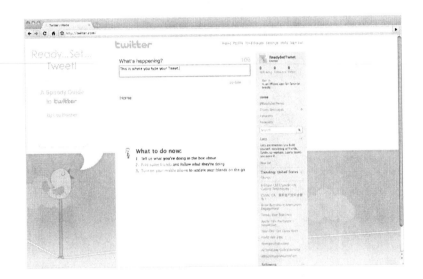

Home Page

Tweets

You will send most of your Tweets from your *Home* page. When you want to send a Tweet:

- Click on *Home*. Type your Tweet (140 characters or less) into the *What's happening?* box at the top of the page.

> **What's happening?** -45
>
> My new book, Ready...Set...Tweet! A speedy guide to Twitter, was just published. Please send me comments after you read it. It tells you what you need to know to get started on Twitter.
>
> update

Explanation:

When you type more than 140 characters in the box, you will see the number of characters you are over at the right-hand side (for example: -45). You will not be able to send your tweet unless you have 140 characters or less in the box.

> **What's happening?** 0
>
> My new book, Ready...Set...Tweet! was just published. Please send me comments after you read it. It tells you how to get started on Twitter.
>
> update

- Click on the *update* button under the box when you are ready to send the Tweet.

> **What's happening?** 140
>
> [   ]
>
> Latest: My new book, Ready...Set...Tweet! was just published. Please send me comments after you read it. It tells you how to get started on Twitter. less than 5 seconds ago
>
> update
>
> **Home**
>
> **ReadySetTweet** My new book, Ready...Set...Tweet! was just published. Please send me comments after you read it. It tells you how to get started on Twitter.
> less than 5 seconds ago from web

- After you click *update*, your Tweet will appear in the stream of Tweets on your page.

Once posted, your Tweet will slowly work its way down the page as other Tweets are added to the page by you or by those you are following. The most recent Tweets are always at the top of the page.

Always put @ before a person's username in a Tweet if you want that person to notice that it is especially aimed at them.

The rest of the page under the box is where Tweets will occur in chronological order in real time with the most recent at the top.

Other items in the Tweet stream

Below following, followers and listed you will see a word defined. This is a feature of Twitter to help you build your Twitter vocabulary.

- **Star** (☆).
  Beside each Tweet is the outline of a *star.* If you like a particular Tweet of someone you are following and want to find it more easily later, you can mark it as a *favorite* by clicking on the *star* beside it. This will save the Tweet in chronological order to your *Favorites* list.

- **Curved arrow** (↰).
  The *curved arrow* next to a Tweet is where you click to *reply* to a Tweet.

Explanation:

When you click on the *curved arrow,* the name of the *What's happening?* box will change to *Reply to their username.* Inside the box, you will see the *@username* of the person to whom you are replying. After the *@username,* you will type your *reply.* You will also notice the *update* button under the box now says *reply.* Click on this button to post the reply. The @ symbol before a username functions to send that Tweet to a list of Tweets on their Twitter site mentioning them. It makes it much easier for the person to find Tweets to and about them.

- **Retweet** (↻ Retweet).
  When you pass your cursor over the area to the right of the *Reply* curved arrow, you will see arrows that form a box. This is the *Retweet* button.

When you click on this button, a box comes up that asks you if you want to *Retweet to your followers?* If you click on *yes,*

the *retweet* will go out to all of your followers. If you decide you did not intend to *retweet* this Tweet, you merely click on the X beside *yes* and the *retweet* will be cancelled.

- **More.**

The bar at the bottom of the page says *more*. Click on this to see Tweets that occurred prior to this page.

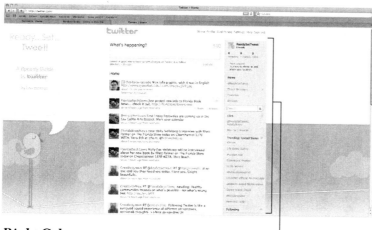

Right Column

The right column (or right sidebar) contains the following items:

- **Your avatar, username and the cumulative number of times you have Tweeted.**

- **Following.**

This is the number of people you are following. If you click on this number, you will see a list of the people who you are following.

- **Followers.**

This is the number of people who are following you. If you click on this number, you will see a list of the people who are following you.

- **Listed.**

  This is a way for people on Twitter to categorize those they follow. For example, I follow lots of artists and writers and photographers, so it would be logical for me to have *Lists* of the favorites of those I follow for each of these categories. This *listed* designation beside *followers* tells you how many other Twitter sites have *listed* your Twitter site. If you click on this number, you will land on a page where you will see a list of the *Lists* following you. There are two tabs on this page. If you click on the tab, *Lists you follow*, you will see a list of the *Lists* you are following.

  Home

- **Home.**

  This is a duplicate of the *Home* button at the top of the page.

- **@yourusername.**

  Click on this item and you will see a list of Tweets that mention your Twitter username.

  Explanation:

  This is the place you will go after several hours being off Twitter. For example, on my site called @LouWrites, if I click on @LouWrites in the right-hand column, I will see a list of all the Tweets that have mentioned @LouWrites. Therefore, if someone replied to one of my tweets, I'll see that reply here and won't have to scroll through all the tweets from the previous few hours. This list will save you a considerable amount of time. Note that there is a *What's happening?* box at the top of this page for your convenience, so you can Tweet back to those who have mentioned you if you are so inclined.

  Direct Messages   1

- **Direct Messages.**

  People who you are following can send you direct messages. Others cannot. If you click on *Direct Messages*, you will see direct messages that others have sent you. Direct messages are private messages between the sender and you. Click *reply* to respond.

Send [▾] a direct message.　　　　　　　　　140

send

Direct messages sent only to you

| Inbox | Sent |

LouWrites d Do you know when the book will be listed on
Amazon.com?
3:07 PM Feb 1st
↩ Reply　Delete

reply to LouWrites

Explanation:

Many people will send you direct messages in order to thank you for
following them or to entice you to go to their website. You can decide
whether you want to respond to these. At other times, people will send
a direct message if they have something they want to tell you privately.
Copies of direct messages are sent to the email address you listed on
your *Account* page if you checked the box on *Notices* to have the emails
forwarded. You cannot respond to them from your email however.

To respond to a direct message, click on the *reply* button at
the right side of the message. There is also a *delete* button at
the right side of the direct message. You are free to use this to
keep your list short or you can just let them accumulate.

Favorites

● Favorites.

This is where you can retrieve the Tweets you have starred as
Favorites. They will be listed here in chronological order.

Retweets

● Retweets.

When you click on *Retweets*, you will land on a page with three
categories. By clicking on one of the three tabs, you will get a list of:

What's happening?   140

Latest: A good way to keep up with changes on Twitter is to follow
@twitter. 1 day ago   update

| Retweets by others | Retweets by you | Your tweets, retweeted |

flashsourcecode Nice info graphic, wish it was in English:
http://www.quentindelobel.com/images/JMB.jpg
about 5 hours ago from web
Retweeted by ninakatz

1. Retweets by others

2. Retweets by you

3. Your tweets, retweeted

Explanation:

Since it's helpful to know if others seem interested enough in your
Tweets to retweet you, it's good to check all three daily. It's also
good to thank those who have retweeted your Tweets. Use the
reply button for this and write your reply in the box at the top of
the page. (Note: There is also a button to retweet a retweet and
then one to undo a retweet of a retweet. Whew! That sounds
confusing, but if you are looking at the retweet page, it will make
sense. Essentially, some Tweets are retweeted and you see it when
it has been retweeted; and it might be such a good Tweet that you
want to retweet it also. This makes it easy for you to do so.)

Next to each Tweet on the *Your tweets, retweeted* tab are two choices,
one is a *star* to mark it as a *Favorite* and the other is a *Delete* button.

| Search | 🔍 |

• Search.

Enter a word here and all recent Tweets
containing that word will come up.

Explanation:

This is handy when looking for people to follow. For example, if you are a scuba diver and are looking for other scuba enthusiasts, put in the word *scuba* and the Tweets will come up that mention *scuba*. In this list of search results, you can click on the usernames of the Tweeters and go to their Profile Twitter pages to see if you might want to follow any of them.

When finished with any of the lists you pull up through the search engine, click on *Home* to return to your *Home* page.

> **Lists** ⌃
>
> @ReadySetTweet/
> helpfulhints
>
> New list | View all

- **Lists.**

  Click on the word *Lists* and you'll see active links to all of your lists and active links to those who have listed you. Click on any of these lists to visit them.

To create your own lists, click on *New list* under *Lists*. You will see *Create a new list* form where you fill in the *List name*, *Description* (a 100-character description of your list) and you choose whether you want the list to be *Public* or *Private* (just for your own use). When you finish creating your list, click on *Create list* and you will land on a page where you can *Find people to add to your list*. You can look through your

following page or search for people to add to the list, or you can use the list feature during the natural course of adding people to follow.

- Trending Worldwide.

  The items listed under *Trending Worldwide* are the topics that Twitter has determined to be popular. By clicking on one, you'll go to a list of Tweets that mention that topic. You can refine this list to local topics by clicking on *Change*, clicking on one of the locations listed, and then clicking on *Done*.

- Following.

  This section of the Home page is where the avatars of those you are following are grouped. You can click on the *view all* button and a complete list of those you are following will come up. (Note

that *view all* will not be visible until you are following at least 37 people.) On this list, you will see icons to the right of each person.

1. One icon looks like a list. Click on this and you will see the names of your lists. For each person you follow, you can click the name(s) of the list(s) you want to add the person to.

2. The other icon to the far right looks like a wheel. Click on this and you will find a list of actions you can take regarding that person. (These items are self-explanatory, but the two of note are: *Unfollow* and *Block*. By clicking *Unfollow*, you can remove someone from the list of people you follow. By clicking on *Block*, you can block someone from following you.) The list includes:

- @ Mention (also reply)
- Direct message
- Unfollow
- Block
- Report for spam

Profile Page

This is the page that visitors see. The whole page contains only your Tweets. Beside each Tweet, you'll see a *star* and a *trash can*. Use the *star* to mark a particular Tweet for any reason. It will appear in your *Favorites* list and will be much easier to find in the future. Use the *trash can* to delete a Tweet. If you delete a Tweet, it is not only deleted from your page, but it is deleted throughout

Twitter.

The right-hand column of the Profile page shows:

- the information (Name, Location, Web, Bio) you uploaded on the *Account* page in *Settings*. It also shows who you are following and your followers and the lists you are on as it does on the *Home* page.

- Tweets.
This is the cumulative number of times you have Tweeted.

- Favorites.
This is where you can retrieve the Tweets you have starred as favorites. They will be listed here in chronological order.

ReadySetTweet's lists

Lists following you 2	Lists you follow 1
@LouWrites/writers	Following: 33 / Followers: 2
@BrevardArtNews/florida	Following: 8 / Followers: 0

- Lists.
Click on the *view all* at the bottom of *Lists* and you'll go to a page with two tabs: *Lists following you* and *Lists you follow*. Click on any list to see the recent Tweets of those on the list. You can also click on the active links to individual lists on your *Profile* page.

You will also see the list icon and the word *Lists* at the top of the tweets directly to the right of *That's you!*

- Following.
This section of the *Profile* page is where the avatars of those you are following are grouped. You can click on the *view all* button and a complete list of those you are following will come up. (Note that *view all* will not be visible until you are following at least 37 people.) On this list, you will see icons to the right of each person.

1. One icon looks like a list. Click on this and you will see the

names of your lists. For each person you follow, you can click the name(s) of the list(s) you want to add the person to.

2. The other icon to the far right looks like a wheel. Click on this and you will find a list of actions you can take regarding that person. (These items are self-explanatory, but the two of note are: *Unfollow* and *Block*. By clicking *Unfollow*, you can remove someone from the list of people you follow. By clicking on *Block*, you can block someone from following you.) The list includes:

   - @ Mention (also reply)

   - Direct message

   - Unfollow

   - Block

   - Report for spam

Find People

There are four ways to search for people, organizations, or businesses on Twitter. First, click on the *Find People* button next to the *Profile* button in the menu bar at the top of the page. This will bring up a *Find accounts and follow them* page. On this page, you'll find the four different ways to search.

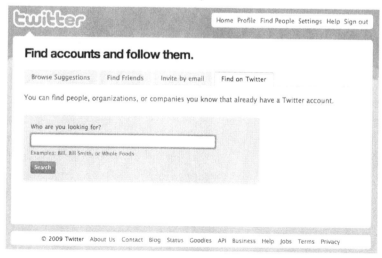

- Find on Twitter

   When you click on *Find People* on your *Home* or *Profile* pages you will land on the *Find on Twitter* page. Type the name of a person in the space provided and click on *Search*. A list of possibilities will come up. Click on the one you think is the person or account you are looking for. Don't be discouraged if your first attempt doesn't work. Sometimes people sign on to Twitter under the name of their blog or under a nickname, so be a little inventive in your search.

- **Invite by email**

  By clicking on *Invite by email*, Twitter provides a space for you to enter email addresses of your friends and associates to find them and invite them to follow you on Twitter. It shows you a sample email that will be sent to each email address you enter, so you can decide if you want to use this feature. Once you have filled in the list, click on *Invite*.

- **Find Friends**

  If you have a gmail, yahoo, or aol account, you can have Twitter search your email address book for people on Twitter by entering your email address and your email password on this page and clicking on the name of the appropriate email provider in the left-hand column.

- **Browse Suggestions**

  If you click on the *Browse Suggestions* tab, you will land on a page with a list of topics. By clicking on a topic of interest to you, you will land on a list of Twitter sites that may be of interest. Click on the ones you want to follow.

Settings

Settings is the next button. We covered this thoroughly when we were setting up your account and your look. Refer to Chapter 7 on this.

Help

Click on the *Help* button when you want information about a specific topic. At the top of the page you land on is a space to type a topic you have a question about. Click on search and it will take you to a list of responses about the topic.

Sign out

When you are finished with your session on Twitter, click on *Sign out* to close
your account until you want to use it again.

Chapter 10:
Tweeting Overview

Writing a Tweet

Types of Tweets

Chapter 10: Tweeting Overview

I know it seems like a lot leading to the point where you are putting out your first Tweet and even though the topic of this section is Tweeting, I'm hoping you will read this chapter for information and hold off on Tweeting until we reach Chapter 12. This chapter is to give you an overview of *Tweets, following,* and *followers.*

Writing a Tweet

All Tweets can be no more than 140 characters. That's a fact, not a suggestion. When you are wanting to Tweet, you will type your message of 140 characters or less into the *What's happening?* box at the top of the *Home* page. There is a counter on this box that will count down the number of characters you have typed into the box. Spaces count as characters, too, so don't be fooled by this. When you reach zero characters, the counter will count in negative numbers -4, -5, etc. You can type your whole message if you want to be sure you don't forget what you were going to write, then begin reducing it to fit the 140-character specification.

For example, let's say you want to Tweet about your new book and you devise a Tweet. Usually we start with too many characters. Here are three versions of a Tweet until it's the right size.

What's happening?	-45

My new book, Ready...Set...Tweet! A speedy guide to Twitter, was just published. Please send me comments after you read it. It tells you what you need to know to get started on Twitter.

update

- First you type: *My new book, Ready...Set...Tweet!: A Speedy Guide to Twitter was just published. Please send me comments after you read it. It tells you what you need to know to get started on Twitter.* This Tweet is 185 characters. The counter on my Tweet tells me that it is -45, so I have to get rid of 45 characters before I can send it.

- I look at that Tweet to see what is expendable. Right off, I see that in the last sentence I can substitute the word "how" for "what you need to know." So, now I have *My new book, Ready...Set...Tweet!: A Speedy Guide to Twitter,was just published. Please send me comments after*

you read it. It tells you how to get started on Twitter. That eliminated 18 characters, so I still have to reduce my tweet by 27 more.

> **What's happening?**   0
>
> My new book, Ready...Set...Tweet! was just published. Please send me comments after you read it. It tells you how to get started on Twitter.
>
> update

- I study the Tweet again, and I notice that I can eliminate quite a few characters if I use just the main portion of the title of the book rather than the extended title. So, I delete ": A Guide to Twitter." And I rearrange a few words to get below 140. My final Tweet says: *Just published my new book, Ready...Set... Tweet! Please send me comments after you read it. It tells you how to get started on Twitter.* That brings me down to 140 characters and I'm ready to Tweet, so I click on the *update* button.

Types of tweets

Usual Tweets

- **Regular Tweet.**

  A regular Tweet is a straight Tweet of 140 characters or less telling your followers something.

  Explanation:

  With this Tweet, you simply type your message into the *What's happening?* box and click on update. My general advice to you is to make your Tweets interesting, informative and easy to read. You will gain followers if you ensure that you write careful Tweets that others will want to read. I'm much more apt to click on the link to someone's website or blog if they tell me something interesting in their Tweets. If you just Tweet what's really happening (such as *I'm going to the store, I'm off to take a nap,* or *I'm bored,* etc.) I won't be as apt to click on your link or to follow you. It's good to have most of your Tweets about the topic of your Twitter page and a few mundane ones thrown in to show your friendliness.

- **Reply.**

  You can reply to any Tweet that catches your eye. To do so, click on the *curved arrow* next to the Tweet. Their Twitter address (*@username*) will appear in the box at the top of the page. Leave a space then type your reply to them. These Tweets also gain followers as they are seen by your followers and the followers of the other person. Some of these people may find you interesting and start following you.

- **Direct message.**

  Use *direct message* when you want to send a private message to one of your followers.

  Explanation:

  Click on *Direct Messages* in the sidebar of your Home page. It will take you to a page with two tabs: *Inbox* and *Sent. Inbox* will show you direct messages sent to you and *Sent* will show you direct messages you have sent.

  You can reply to a direct message you have received by clicking on the *Reply* button (curved arrow) to the right side of it. You'll see the *username* of the person you are sending the direct message to in the box at the top of the page. Merely type your reply in the box provided and click on *send*.

  To initiate and send a direct message, type *d username* then the message you want to send to a follower in the box at the top of the page if you have not sent or received a direct message from that person before. If you have sent or received a direct message from the person before, they will be listed in the drop-down menu above the Tweet box. Click on their name and then write your message in the box. Your direct message will look something like this: *d creativitynow I like your blog post from yesterday. I'd like to email you about it. Is that possible?*

> You can only send direct messages (d) to your followers. Don't frustrate yourself by trying to send them to others.

Specialty Tweets

- **Tweet including a link to your website or blog.**

    Explanation:

    When you post something to your blog or to your website, good use of Twitter is to Tweet about the new posting. This will draw immediate attention to it. So, when you post something to your blog or website, put out a Tweet including the link to the blog or website. This will alert others that you have something new and will give them easy access to it.

    For example, when I post something about a specific gallery, I might post a Tweet saying, *Just posted a call for artists from the XYZ Gallery. See details: http://brevardartnews. com.* (Unlike other places, you must use http:// when you are including a link in a Tweet or the link will not work.)

    If the URL of the website you are putting in your Tweet is long, you may want to shrink it. Do this by opening another browser window and going to *http://TinyURL.com.* Type or paste the long URL in the box labeled *Enter a long URL to make tiny,* click on *Make tinyURL!* The tiny URL is saved to your clipboard. Go back to your Twitter page and enter the tiny URL into the Tweet by pasting it using control-v (for pc users) or command-v (for Mac users).

- **Tweet a picture.**

    You can easily Tweet a link to a picture and its caption. Here's how:

    1. To Tweet a picture, open another browser and go to *http://twitpic.com.*

    2. *Login* using your Twitter *username* and *password* then click on *Login.*

    3. To put up a picture, click on the *Upload Photo* button in the upper right side of the page.

    4. Browse your hard drive for the picture you want to display.

    5. When you find the picture, click on it, then click *Open.* This will upload the picture to Twitpic.

6. Next, include something to say about the picture. This will become your Tweet.

7. Click on *upload* and you're done. You have just Tweeted the picture and your comment to Twitter.

Explanation:
The Twitpic URL for your picture will occur in your Tweet. Hopefully, some of your followers will click on the URL and comment on the picture. Their comments become Tweets as well, and the Twitpic URL for that picture goes out with the comment. Therefore, their followers see the URL and may go see the picture and become interested in following you. It's a good way to gain some attention from others.

- **Tweet with a link to an interesting website or video.**
Don't make your Tweets just about you. If you find a wonderful website, share it with others. Also, you may want to share a video through Youtube.com. Just type the URL of the website where you want your readers to land (starting with http://) into the Tweet. For example, my Tweet might be, *Just found a great site for Brevard artists. See it at http://www.artsbrevard.org.*

- **Retweet (RT).**
The retweet button is to the right of all Tweets. Click on it and you will see a small box that will ask you if you want to send that Tweet to all of your followers. Click *yes* if you want to send it.

Explanation:
With a retweet, you are telling others that you admire the Tweet you are sending. You see Tweets of the people you are following, but your followers don't see them. So by retweeting a Tweet, you are sending someone else's Tweet out to your followers. The original Tweeter will probably thank you for the RT. This will give you an opportunity to start a conversation with this person if you want. And the *thank you* will go out to their followers who might notice you. Are you beginning to see how the networking on Twitter works? Try to interact with others as much as you can.

Another way to retweet is by pasting a tweet into the *What's happening?* box on the Home page. At the beginning of the Tweet, put *RT* to mark it as a retweet and then *@username* to show who originally sent the Tweet. If you still have room in the 140-character limit, you can say why you are retweeting it. When you add your comment to a retweet, use brackets to enclose what you are saying. Here's an example of a retweet: *RT @sharks Great website about sharks. http://sharkexample.com {Great Pictures. Go see them}*

What's happening? 46

RT @sharks Great website about sharks. http://sharkexample.com {Great Pictures. Go see them}|

Latest: Tweet Tip: Change the colors of your text by going to Settings then Design and clicking on Change design colors. #TweetTip about 11 hours ago

update

Ready...Set...Tweet! A Speedy Guide to Twitter

Chapter 11:
Followers and Following

**Basic: Find followers using
Twitter's integrated tools**

**Beyond Basic: Other ways to
find followers**

Chapter 11: Followers and Following

If you don't follow and find folks to follow you, you will just sit on Twitter Tweeting to yourself. You might eventually find a follower or two when someone just happens to search for a word that's in one of your Tweets, but you won't find many without going out and following others. So, let's get busy and find someone for you to follow.

Basic: Find Followers Using Twitter's Integrated Tools

This section is to familiarize you with following and followers. Don't do anything yet. Learn the concepts here. The reason I caution you to not start following until you are completely ready is that if your page is not completely set up, those you follow who come to see your Twitter page will find nothing and may not follow you back. So sit back and read this complete section, then we'll get started.

You can follow others, but you can't gather followers. What this means is that you can click on the *follow* button on a Twitter page you like, but you can't make that person follow you back. They'll have to make that decision on their own. More often than not, if you follow people who happen to be interested in your topic and you make your Twitter page and Tweets interesting, they will follow you back.

Find People

We talked about this earlier. The *Find People* button is next to the *Profile* button at the top of your Twitter page. To save you from having to look back to the section where I described how to use the *Find People* feature, I'll repeat that section here.

There are four ways to search for people, organizations, or businesses on Twitter. First, click on the *Find People* button next to the *Profile* button in the menu bar at the top of the page. This will bring up a *Find accounts and follow them* page. On this page, you'll find the four different ways to search.

- Find on Twitter.
  When you click on *Find People* on your *Home* or *Profile* pages you will land on the *Find on Twitter* page. Type the name of a person

in the space provided and click on *Search*. A list of possibilities will come up. Click on the one you think is the person or account you are looking for. Don't be discouraged if your first attempt doesn't work. Sometimes people sign on to Twitter under the name of their blog or under a nickname, so be a little inventive in your search.

- Invite by email.

  By clicking on *Invite by email*, Twitter provides a space for you to enter email addresses of your friends and associates to find them and invite them to follow you on Twitter. It shows you a sample email that will be sent to each email address you enter, so you can decide if you want to use this feature. Once you have filled in the list, click on *Invite*.

- Find Friends.

  If you have a gmail, yahoo, or aol account, you can have Twitter search your email address book for people on Twitter by entering your email address and your email password on this page and clicking on the name of the appropriate email provider in the left-hand column.

- Browse Suggestions.

  If you click on *Browse Suggestions*, you will land on a page with a list of topics. By clicking on a topic of interest to you, you will land on a list of Twitter sites that may be of interest. Click on the ones you want to follow.

Beyond Basic: Other Ways to Find Followers

Using following to find people to follow.
Once you find someone—even just one person—to follow, you're in business. Through that person you will have the possibility of finding more. Here's how to do it:

- Click on the word *following* close to the top in the sidebar column on the Twitter page of a person you are following. A list of the people that person is following will come up.

- Click on the *username* or avatar of someone who looks interesting to you. You will land on their Profile page.

- Take a look at their bio and determine if you have an interest in

following them. Also, it might help to look at their Tweets or go to their website or blog to see if you are interested in following them.

- If you decide you are interested, click on the word *Follow* (on the left side of the page under their avatar) on their Profile page, and they will be added to those you follow.

Outside help through Tweepsearch.

- Open your Twitter site then minimize it.

- Open another browser and go to *http://tweepsearch.com*.

- On the front page of *tweepsearch.com* is a space to type a key word or words of interest to you. Put that word or words in that space.

Tweepsearch. com is helpful in finding people to follow. It searches for Twitter users by the words in their bios.

Explanation:
By entering two or more words with commas between them you can make your search more specific. For example, you may be a scuba diver and put in a search for *scuba*. The result of that search will probably be quite a list. If you are in Hawaii and want to connect with others in Hawaii who are interested in scuba, then enter the words *scuba* and *Hawaii* into the search engine (enter them as follows "scuba, Hawaii"). The result of that search will be more specific. It will yield people who have "scuba" and "Hawaii" entered in their bios.

- Now you have a list of people on Twitter who have an interest in scuba and Hawaii. To use this list, click on the @username of someone on the list, and you will go to their Twitter page where you can apply your criteria to decide whether you want to follow them or not.

- Click on the *Follow* button if you want to follow. Then, close the person's Twitter page to return to your list on *tweepsearch.com* and try the next. You can repeat the process with different words any time you want by putting the words into the search engine at the top of the page.

Following through the Tweets of others.

Another good way to find people to follow is by reading the Tweets of those you follow. Watch them for the mention of other people who you don't follow. When you see an interesting conversation, click on the @username of the person they are talking to and check out that person's bio and blog or website. If you think you

are interested in them, then follow them.

- **Search.**

    Use the search bar in the right column of the Home page and put in specific words. We talked about this before, but I'll repeat it here so you don't have to thumb back through the book.

    Enter a word here and all recent tweets containing that word will come up. This is handy when looking for people to follow. For example, if you are a scuba diver and are looking for other scuba enthusiasts, put in the word *scuba* and recent Tweets will come up that mention *scuba*. In this list of the results to your search, you can click on the usernames of individuals and go to their Twitter pages.

- **Hashtag.**

    The pound or number sign — # — is called hashtag on Twitter. Using a word with a hashtag on the front of it is a way to catalog your Tweets so they will be seen by others who use the same symbol. For example, if I write a Tweet about writing and want it to be seen by others who mark their Tweets about writing, I will put #writing at the end of the Tweet. After I Tweet, I can click on #writing in my Tweet. Twitter will bring up a list of all the recent Tweets with #writing in them. You can use hashtags to find people of like interest to follow.

- **#followfriday.**

    It's customary on Fridays for people to Tweet about those who they follow who they recommend for others to follow. To join this custom, write a Tweet listing the @usernames of a couple of people you enjoy following. Put the word *#followFriday* in the Tweet and a reason you recommend people follow them. For example, if someone wanted to recommend that others follow @*floridabooknews* and @*brevardartnews*, they would do it like this:

    #followFriday @brevardartnews @floridabooknews Follow both of these sites for news on the arts and books in Florida.

    Some people cram 6 or 8 people to follow into one Tweet. I don't recommend this. Make yours meaningful by including only a couple names and saying why people should follow them. They

Attract people to follow you by Tweeting great content. Remember: Tweets should be interesting, valuable, and entertaining.

will Tweet back and you might get some meaningful support going. In addition to #followFriday, different professions have days that they Tweet about each other, such as #writersWednesday, #travelThursday, etc. Watch for this with your topic and join in. It's a great way to get to know other Tweeters.

Chapter 12:
Get Started by Putting it all Together

Set up your site

Start Tweeting

Next: Find some people to follow

A quick review of following and followers

Your daily Twitter routine

Scheduling your tweets

A bit of advice

Chapter 12: Get Started by Putting it all Together

There is a method to all this. I have told you throughout to hold off on Tweeting until we could put it all together. We are ready to do that. Follow these steps to get started *following*, *gathering followers* and *Tweeting on Twitter*.

Set up your site

By now, your Twitter site should be set up. If you didn't set it up as you read through the instructions, go back and set it up now.

Before you start gathering followers and Tweeting, it is important to have your Twitter site looking the way you want. People will judge whether they want to follow you by the information on your site.

Also, if you are setting up a Twitter site in order to drive traffic to your website or blog, it's good to concentrate on setting up your website or blog first, so you are ready to present a positive image to visitors.

> Be sure your blog or website is looking good before you start Tweeting on Twitter. People will be visiting it.

Once you have all of that set up, and once you have your Twitter site looking the way you want with a good background, your avatar, your one-line bio and the URL for your blog in place, devise four or five Tweets about yourself and about your interests. The first Tweet could be that you just joined Twitter and are excited to get going. A couple more Tweets could describe what your interests are. And one of the Tweets could take people to your blog. That's a good mixture to get started. For example:

- I'm new to Twitter. I'm glad to be Tweeting at last.

- I'm currently writing a book about Twitter. It's coming along nicely. Will Tweet quotes from it later.

- I'm interested in all types of writing and in publishing as a whole. I blog about writing and give people tips on writing.

- Visit my blog to see my writing interests. *http://WritersCreativeStudio.com*

Start Tweeting

Once you start Tweeting, you'll need to keep Tweeting to ensure your site looks active. So pick a time to start your Twitter site when you have time to devote some attention to it.

Send out your four or five Tweets to the Twitter world. Remember, do not feel bad if no one responds to you. After all, no one is following you at this point. These Tweets are to have something on your Profile page to show the people you start following that you are worth following back.

Next: Find some people to follow

Implement the strategies you learned in the previous chapter to find people to follow. Be picky enough with whom you follow to have interesting Tweets to read and to respond to, but don't be so picky that it takes you more than a few minutes (like 4 or 5 at the most) to decide whether to follow each individual. When you find someone you want to follow, click on the *Follow* button on their Twitter page and their Tweets will start to flow into your Home page.

You may be startled at first because the Tweets of the first person you follow will fill the page. This is normal and is only because you are only following one person. It doesn't mean they are sending out Tweets every couple of seconds. As you follow more and more people, the Tweets will occur in real time and you will see a variety of Tweets, including your own on the page.

When you follow others, a certain percentage of them will follow you back. Depending on what you specified under *Notices*, you will receive an email each time someone follows you. You will probably receive direct messages from some of these people also, inviting you to go to their websites, etc.

As you follow more and more, others will notice you following people who you have in common and will start following you too. When people who you are not following start following you, you will receive an email. When you receive these emails from people you are not following, you can click on the link in the email and visit their Twitter page and decide whether you want to follow them or not. Remember it's up to you. You don't need to follow everyone who is following you.

When I read these emails, I act on them and delete them. Your are free to make

your own decision on whether to save the emails or to delete them. After a few days or a month, you'll probably be wanting to delete them because you'll have quite a few.

Throughout the whole following process, remember to continue Tweeting and interacting with others on Twitter to maintain the interest of your followers.

A quick review of following and followers

- Use the *Find People* button at the top of the Twitter page to find people to follow.
- Look at the *following* lists of those you are following and follow the ones that are of interest to you.
- Go to *Tweepsearch.com* and search for people to follow by topics and location.
- Click on people mentioned in the Tweets of others and follow them if interested.
- Use the search engine in the right column of your Twitter site to search for people through the topics they Tweet.
- Click on a word with # (hashtag) in it to find people Tweeting about your topic.
- Watch for #followFriday recommendations from people you enjoy following.

Your daily Twitter routine

Once you have set up your Twitter site and have started Tweeting and finding people to follow, it'll be easiest if you set up a Twitter routine. Here are some things to consider when establishing a routine.

How often you Tweet and how much time you put into your research will depend on your schedule. If you can only spend a bit of time in the morning on Twitter, then you need to make the most of your time. For example, you could spend a few minutes on Google searching for a couple of key words that pertain to your blog and the people you are trying to attract to follow you. Find a couple of nice website links to send in your Tweets. And, note a picture you might

want to throw up on *twitpic.com*. By doing this, you will have information ready to infuse variety into your Tweets to keep the interest and interaction of those following you.

Sometimes, the Tweets will flow. At other times, you'll stare at the screen and nothing will come to mind. To keep from having Tweeter's Block, it's a good idea to keep a little notebook with you and jot down ideas for Tweets when they come to you.

There is no right number of Tweets per day. However, here's a key: Those who are deciding to follow you will be looking at your Profile page to make that decision. So, when you sign out of Twitter, be sure to take a moment to check your Profile page. If it looks as if you haven't been paying much attention lately, you know you'll have to Tweet a little more often.

You can go too far the other way too. You don't want to Tweet so often that it irritates others. Space your Tweets. It's annoying to your followers to receive ten Tweets from you at one time. Most often when I see this on my Home page, I just skip them all.

Scheduling your tweets

I am self-employed, so I'm usually able to Tweet several times per day. If you are unable to do this because you are away from your computer for most of the day, you can schedule your Tweets by using one of several applications. I Tweet using *Hootsuite.com*. There are other applications you can use. I'm not pushing Hootsuite. It's just the one I use and will describe it here to let you know that there are applications out there you can use to save time.

By using Hootsuite.com, I can schedule some of my Tweets to go out throughout the day when I'm not able to be at the computer. With this, I write Tweets early in the morning and schedule them to be Tweeted later. It's probably wise to make them the Tweets that lead people to websites or are quotes that people might find interesting.

I have several blogs and a Twitter account for each one, so this takes me a bit of time in the morning, but it's worth the time. On days when I'm home, I'm active on Twitter while I'm doing other work. Often this activity is through Hootsuite

as well, because I can see all four Twitter sites without logging in and out.

At the end of the day, I always check to see if I have been mentioned and if I need to respond to any direct messages. I do those things promptly, because with the speed of Twitter, there is no way people will remember the thread of the conversation for more than a day.

So, *my routine goes like this:*

- In the morning, I load up Hootsuite with Tweets for the day.

- Before I leave all my Twitter sites to be managed by Hootsuite, I do some personal Tweeting on each site.

- I read the Tweets of others and if I honestly find them interesting, I'll enter into the conversation for a bit. If not, I'll retweet a Tweet or two by others. That helps you to build a network on Twitter. In all cases, I try to be personable and make the most of my live time on Twitter.

- I repeat this routine at the end of the day.

- I'll go over the Tweets of the day that were directed at me and will respond to the ones that seem to hit home.

- For the most part, it's great to Tweet in real time. That means that you Tweet back when the Tweet comes in. Since we've established that that's not always possible, don't worry about responding late to a Tweet that comes your way during the day. We all expect that and don't take offense.

A bit of advice:

I'm sure I said this earlier, but I'll leave you with this hint on how to be successful...

Be generous with information, with your Tweets and with your interest and you'll be successful on Twitter. If you Tweet only about yourself, people will lose interest. However, if you mix it up and make your Tweets about your topics and about the interests of other Tweeters, you will have a better chance of gathering followers and gathering interest on Twitter. So, send out some pictures, send along some links to websites that you find interesting, ask a question now and then, send out a meaningful quote that might be of interest to others, reply to the

Twitter is open for business 24/7. Don't just Tweet at the same time each day. You're missing many opportunities if you do.

Tweets of others, and then once in a while send your followers to your website or blog. You'll be successful if you are interesting and interested as well.

Happy Tweeting to All.

Resources:

Books

Comm, Joel. *Twitter Power: How to Dominate Your Market One Tweet at a Time.* Wiley, 2009.

Evans, Dale. *Social Media Marketing: an Hour a Day.* Cybex, 2008.

O'Reilly, Tim. *The Twitter Book.* O'Reilly Media, 2009.

Safko, Lon, and David K. Brake. *The Social Media Bible: Tactics, Tools, and Strategies for Business Success.* Wiley, 2009.

Zarella, Dan. *The Social Media Marketing Book.* O'Reilly Media, 2009.

Web addresses

bit.ly/
site to convert a long web address into a short one

TinyURL.com
site to convert a long web address into a short one

Tweepsearch.com
searches for key words in the bios of Twitter users

Twitpic.com
site to send out pictures with your Tweets

twitter-resources.com
list of resources for Twitter

twitterbackgroundsgallery.com/resources/
list of resources for Twitter

www.twitip.com/
tutorials on starting on Twitter

wiredpen.com/resources/twitter-resources/
includes Twitter shorthand, tutorials, utilities, search information

Twitter addresses

@twitter
the official Twitter site of Twitter

@readysettweet
the site of *Ready...Set...Tweet!* on Twitter

@lonsafko
co-author of *The Social Media Bible*

@DavidKBrake
co-author of *The Social Media Bible*

@joelcomm
author of *Twitter Power*

Glossary: Terminology You'll Find Helpful

Account: The Account page is where you fill in the information that will go on your Profile page. Click on *Settings* on your Home page and you will land on the *Account* page.

Avatar: A small picture that represents you. It can be an actual picture of you or a picture or icon that represents you.

Background: The design of your page is comprised of the background and foreground. You can change your background by clicking on *Settings* then clicking on *Design*.

Bio (One-line bio): You fill in your one-line bio on the *Account* page. Your one-line bio might include why you are on Twitter, your interests, and what you will be Tweeting about.

Block: If someone follows you and you don't want them as a follower, you can block them. To do this, click on your list of *followers* and find the person you want to block. Click on the icon farthest to the right and click on *Block*.

Delete your account: If you decide to get rid of your Twitter site, click on *Settings*. You will land on your *Account* page. Go to the bottom left corner of the page and click on *Delete my account*.

Design: Click on *Settings* then click on *Design*. The Design page is where you can change your background or the colors of the sidebar, borders, text, and links.

Design colors: You can change the colors of the text, links, sidebar, and sidebar border by clicking on *Change design colors*.

Direct message: A direct message is a private message sent to you by someone you follow or a private message you send to someone who follows you.

Email: You can change the email address you use for your Twitter account on the Account page. Click on *Settings* and you will land on the Account page.

Favorites: You can mark individual Tweets as your favorites by clicking on the star shape to the right of the Tweet. You can find a list of your favorites by clicking on *Favorites* in the sidebar on the Home page.

Find people: Click on *Find People* in the menu bar at the top of the pages and you will land on a page with tabs for four ways to find people to follow.

Followers: These are the people who follow your Tweets on Twitter.

#followFriday: On Fridays, many people recommend other Tweeters who they appreciate by mentioning them in a Tweet with the word #followFriday in it. This means that the Tweeter recommends that others follow those mentioned.

Following: The word Following leads to the list of people the Tweeter is following.

Hashtag: Using a word with a hashtag (#) in front of it in a Tweet

lets you categorize the Tweet by that word. For example *#writing* will take you to a list of Tweets where Tweeters have marked their Tweets with the same hashtag word. Marking Tweets this way helps the Tweeters who are also interested in that category find Tweets of interest to them.

Help: The *Help* button will take you to the help area where you can type in a term or a question. The search engine will pull up information about that term or question.

Home: This is the page on your Twitter site where you will Tweet and see all the Tweets of those you follow.

Hootsuite: Hootsuite.com is a site where you can schedule Tweets to be sent out when you're not at the computer. It's also a place where you can work on multiple Twitter sites without starting and stopping.

Lists: You can categorize those you follow by putting them on lists, and those who follow you can put you on their lists. Lists help you find Tweeters by specific topic.

Location: Location is an item on your Profile page. If you don't want to list your actual location, you can leave that space blank when you fill in the form on your Account page or you can put in a non-specific location, such as The World.

Notices: The Notices page is where you choose what types of notices you want to receive from Twitter. You'll find the page by clicking on *Settings*.

Password: You'll need to choose a password when you sign in. You can change your password on the Password page.

Picture: Your picture on Twitter is called an avatar. Go to *Settings* then click on *Picture* to upload a picture to be your avatar.

Profile: Your Profile page is the page that visitors to your Twitter site will see. It contains your Tweets in chronological order as well as your URL, your location and your one-line bio.

Protected Tweets: Some people protect their Tweets. This means that their Twitter site is only open to those who they allow to see it. If you have a reason to protect your Tweets, you can do so on the Account page.

Retweet: When you retweet, you send out a Tweet again. This could be your Tweet or a Tweet by some-one else. The retweet button is next to the reply button beside each Tweet. The word retweet also occurs in the sidebar on the Home page. Click on this to see recent retweets.

Search: Put topics in the search engine in the sidebar and click enter. You will see real-time results of Tweets containing the topic of your search.

Settings: Click on *Settings* and you will land on the page with tabs for Account, Password, Mobile, Notices, Picture and Design. All of these tabs help you in setting up your Twitter page.

Sign out: Be sure to click on *Sign Out* in the upper right-hand corner

of your Twitter page when you are finished on Twitter for the day.

Trending Worldwide: Trending Worldwide topics are listed in the sidebar on the Home page. These are topics that Twitter has determined to be popular.

Tweepsearch: Tweepsearch at http://tweepsearch.com is a search engine. You enter a word or words and it will search Twitter users for these words in their user bios.

Tweet: A Tweet is the 140-character message you send out from your Twitter page or you receive from others on your Twitter page.

Tweet reply: This is a Tweet that you make in response to a Tweet that catches your eye or a Tweet directed at you.

Tweet with picture: By using Twit-pic.com, you can Tweet a picture with a caption.

Tweet with website: By including the URL of a website in a Tweet, you can send your followers to your website or blog or to a website or blog you find interesting.

Twitter.com: Twitter.com is a place to communicate, share, inform and/or entertain like-minded people through 140-character messages.

Unfollow: If you have chosen to follow someone and decide that you don't want to follow them after all, you can unfollow them. To do this, click on your list of the people you are following and find the person you want to unfollow. Click on the icon farthest to the right and click on *Unfollow.*

URL: This is the Internet address for a website, blog or for your Twitter site.

Username: This is the name used by a Tweeter on Twitter.

Uses for Twitter: Marketing, research, friendship, family, clubs, attention, announcements, collaboration, schedules, etc.

Index:

CPSIA information can be obtained at www.ICGtesting.com
234744LV00003B/40/P